Devil Dogs

Devil Dogs and Jarheads

Victor W. Pearn

Busca, Inc.
Ithaca, New York

Busca, Inc.
P.O. Box 854
Ithaca, NY 14851
Ph: 607-546-4247
Fax: 607-546-4248
E-mail:
info@buscainc.com
www.buscainc.com

First Edition

Printed in the United States of America

ISBN: 0-9666196-3-3

The poems of the present work appeared in *American Western Song:
Poems from 1976 to 2001,* Xlibris Corporation, copyright © 2000 by
Victor W. Pearn. They have undergone significant revision for the
current work, *Devil Dogs and Jarheads.*

Cover design by Steven G. King and Terry Orin of Colorado Art &
Design Co., Boulder.
With thanks to February and Kipp Johnson.

For Sara and Bud Grounds, without whose help and encouragement from the beginning I couldn't have written this book. Thank you for your prayers, support, and love.

Contents

Preface

The first draft of *Devil Dogs and Jarheads,* originally called Marine Basic, was completed in 1996. In 1969 I received my draft notice. I was nineteen years old and working in a one-hundred-year-old clothing factory in Jacksonville, Illinois. My sister Sara had once lived at Ft. Leonardwood, Missouri, with her husband Bud, an Army sergeant. While visiting them I saw enough of that base to lose interest in the Army.

I went to the Air Force, Navy, and Marine recruiters. The Marines would let me enlist for three years and send me to school to become a radio repairman. The other branches had too long of a waiting list. If the Army drafted me I felt certain I would go to Ft. Leonardwood and be blue-tagged for Vietnam after basic training.

The Marines flew me from St. Louis to San Diego for boot camp. After I arrived there, and all the experiences in boot camp, and the following three years repairing Marine Corps radios, became my inspiration for writing *Devil Dogs and Jarheads.* Being a Marine was such a vivid, positive life experience for me. I enjoyed the adventure. In 1972 I was promoted to corporal. When I left the Corps, the Marines gave me an honorable discharge in San Francisco and flew me home.

I had been stationed in San Diego for one year of electronics school. Then I spent one year at Camp Pendleton, and my last year at Kaneohe Bay, Hawaii. Being a Marine was also a nonstop education.

I was sent to noncommissioned officers' training school; nuclear, biological, and chemical warfare school; human relations school; became an expert rifleman; went with six thousand other Marines on ship from Hawaii to southern California for a beachhead assault and went back to Hawaii. I was on a Navy LSD and an LST.

I was sent to Army generator school at Schofield, Hawaii, and I stayed in an Army hospital, Tripler General, where my left kidney was removed. All the doctors and nurses wanted me to stay and transfer into the Army and work at the hospital, but I went back to the Marines. I also took my first college course in sociology, a correspondence course through the University of Michigan.

I matriculated at Lincoln Land Community College in Springfield, Illinois. The State of Illinois provided a four-year military scholarship for me to any state college or university in Illinois. The federal government also helped with the GI Bill. Always in my heart was the desire to go to college.

The Marines let me out six weeks early to start college on time. In the Corps I learned to study and developed self-discipline, confidence, and self-esteem. I was excited about being out of the Marines and living out my college dream. I remember getting goose bumps everyday walking to school thinking about how my dreams were coming true. I was the first person from my family to go to college.

I began writing poetry in 1971 stationed at Kaneohe Bay. I published my first poems the following year as a college freshman in our school paper, *The Lamp*. I skipped my sophomore year and transferred to the University of Illinois at Springfield. John Knoepfle, a poet who was teaching there, enlightened me on the subject of how hard it is in creative writing to write a good poem. I had a double major studying poetry and anthropology. I loved writing so much I used to write papers for other students just for the fun of writing.

In the summer of 1976 I graduated and went to a writer's conference in Boulder at Colorado University. Four years later I matriculated at CU in the Graduate Creative Writing Program and earned my M.A. in writing poetry. Since my first poems were published I have seen the steady publication of my poetry in magazines and newspapers.

In November 2000 I published the poems in *Devil Dogs and Jarheads* myself in a 387-page book, *American Western Song*, under the subtitle of "Marine Basic." I began marketing the book myself, and in June 2001 I exhibited my book at the American Library Association National Conference in San Francisco. A good friend, Charles Pacheco, went with me to help me at my table. Of forty-five hundred exhibitors and twenty thousand librarians I was the only person there with just one book to exhibit. I met Michael Cooper, president of Busca, Inc., and made a business deal with Robert L. Sibert, president of a book bindery in Jacksonville, Illinois. It's a small world. I also met George M. Eberhart, who wrote the first review of my book.

In January 2002 I attended the mid-winter ALA meeting in New Orleans, and Michael Cooper purchased a copy of my book and read part of it in the hotel. The next day he asked me questions about "Marine Basic"; he wanted to know what happened to one of my drill instructors, Sergeant Baker. I shared with Michael that when I write a poem I always try to combine truth with beauty. In that poem, "Orders," I say I don't know what happened to Sgt. Baker and to this day I don't.

When I returned to Boulder I sent an email thanking Michael for buying my book and expressing an interest in my work. A friend of mine, Jerry Gibson, told me he read the book twice and thought I should publish "Marine Basic" as a separate book. I offered it to Michael with the title *Devil Dogs and Jarheads*, and he accepted the project.

When I was nineteen and began my journey in the Marine Corps my mind was better than a camera because I absorbed not only all the sights, sounds, and action, but also I could feel, taste, and get the scent of the whole experience recorded with all the power of my mind and my heart.

In 1996, when I had developed the writing skills I needed to express the poetry of my journey, I found that I awoke each morning with an incredible clarity as if the whole experience had occurred to me yesterday. I wrote most of the first part in the spring, and the second and third in the late fall and early winter. More recently, while preparing *Devil Dogs and Jarheads,* there have been various revisions.

People ask who should read this book. Anybody that has been in the military, and anyone on active duty right now, and all those who will be in the military need to read this book. It will give them a deep understanding about what military life is like stripped of all the trappings, pomp, and ceremony seen on the drill field. Non-military readers can also benefit from the experiences conveyed in these poems. I sincerely hope you get as much from reading this book as I have put into writing it.

Victor W. Pearn
July 2002

Acknowledgement

The author and publisher wish to gratefully acknowledge the generous assistance of Major General Donald R. Gardner, U.S. Marine Corps (Ret), Chief Executive Officer of Marine Corps University Foundation, Inc. General Gardner's insightful reading of these poems, coupled with constructive feedback, contributed significantly to *Devil Dogs and Jarheads.*

Donald R. Gardner

Marine Basic

in memory of John Montreuil

Phase One

Drill Instructor
in a Smoky the Bear Hat

He just got back from Viet Nam. His green eyes have
red flames in them. Staff Sergeant Butler, one of our
DI's, crams his lion chest out wearing gold wings; the
emblem of Marines who are recon men. Four in his fire
team dropped behind enemy lines by parachute to survey
the area, count Chinese officers, North Korean Marines,
and Viet Cong. He has old tales to tell raw recruits
lurking late until his lungs expand neck veins pop up
his cocoa butter tan face grimaces, "Get your ASS on
the yellow footprints.

Yellow Footprints

Comical yellow footprints.
Find a pair and stand on them.
The DI wants us to do that,
obligingly you find a place.

An hundred-fifteen pound DI
screams at a 300 pound recruit
wants him on the footprints too,
but the big guy challenges.

Two hard quick punches
to the soft stomach.
The bantamweight gamecock DI
wins, in the first round.

No gloating here. The big guy
on the footprints grips his gut.
It is past midnight
and a dozen DIs huddle.

We are not in uniforms yet,
and we do not know how to march.
Under starlight we stand silently
wondering what will happen to us.

This is humorous and serious,
when the DIs break we are ushered
single file and every recruit
passes through the door.

When it is your turn you are told
to quickly enter through the door
and sit in the first chair you find.
This all happens with blinding speed,

within the first thirty seconds.
Never again will you stand on yellow
footprints, but you will remember
their color for the rest of your life.

Barber Chairs

Clippers humming
a barbershop quartet.

In the tradition
a long row of chairs.

One style for all mirrors
a thirty second haircut.

For all those hours
and you have joined.

Receiving

After you sprint
from the barber chair
you come to a long counter.
Great shouting
down the halls:
what is your waist size,
your shoe size?
Somebody throws a sea bag
green socks fly at you
belts, T shirts, boxer shorts,
all the articles of clothing
you will need for the next 12 weeks.
If you get the wrong size
too bad, tough shit, wear them.

Then the herd
stampedes into a room
with cubical desks.
You are given a box,
take off your civilian
clothes, put them into
the box, and address
the box to your home.
This is your last chance
to get rid of any contraband,
guns, knives, drugs you may
have brought with you without
getting into trouble.
It is the last time
you will see that box.

Get your group shower.
Gold dial soap bars
five shower heads
blast steam, duck under,
lather up, rinse off,
get out, drip dry, try on
your new boxer shorts,
T shirt, green utility pants
and socks, black basketball shoes,
gray sweatshirt, put on your hat
grab your sea bag and run
out the door. Everybody waiting.

The sea bag on your shoulder
might weigh 60 pounds.
The DI wants you to
form four lines.
The tallest man
in front. The shortest man
in the rear of the line.
Now put your left hand
on the shoulder of the
man in front of you,
and lock your right arm
around the left arm
of the man to your right.
Now walk and stagger
like a million legged
caterpillar.

Nobody knows how to march,
but somehow you finally
reach your assigned quarters.

Metal bunkbeds, wooden footlockers,
pick a bed, put your sea bag
into the footlocker.

You are given two green wool
blankets, two sheets, a pillow
a pillowcase, and the soft spoken
DI demonstrates how
to make your bed with
military folds,
expects you to
make your rack
like that,
gives you ten minutes
to make your bed.
And when he returns
your rack made,
you will be
standing at attention
in your skivvies.

The angry
green and red eyed
Drill Instructor
comes in yelling
to get your covers off.
"Take off those covers,"
everybody starts ripping
blankets and throwing them
on the floor.
Angry DI throws people
on the floor, anybody
he can get his hands on.
Then he grabs a recruit,
pulls his hat off and says,
"ladies this is your cover
and you better have
those racks made
before the other DI
gets back."

Soft spoken DI
comes in. Your bed is made.
You are at attention
in your skivvies.
He checks arms, legs, backs
for bruises, wounds,
broken bones, to be sure
we are healthy,
then tells us to get in bed.
At the light switch
he says, "there are armed
guards outside the door
with orders to shoot anybody
that tries to escape,"
then he turns out the lights.
"Good night ladies."
It is 3 a.m.

First Night Floor is Deck

Nomenclature
in the Marine Corps:
hat is a *cover*,
bathroom is a *head*,
Drill Instructor is a *DI*,
and we have become *ladies*.

Thoughts swirling
in your brain,
you have lived through
a worse nightmare
than you ever
dreamed possible.

You asked for it.
You enlisted.
This is temporary.
This will pass.
What is the best way to survive?
Go through it. You will make it.

If you can call two hours sleep
a night. That first night
calm, silent, peaceful,
your eyes close, mind slows,
then you hear Gabriel
sounding his trumpet.

"Take What You Want But Eat What You Take"

—sign on the chow hall

Nobody gets up this early,
not tough birds
not sea gulls.
Starlight at morning chow.

March in stand at attention
take your hat off
ignore the aroma
as you go in the door,
pick up a metal tray
sidestep, sidestep,
hold your tray out
for food you want.
Everyday the same
shit on a shingle.

Toast, chipped beef, gravy,
and eggs turning green.

In lunch line I am talking.
Have I forgotten my manners?
No, I am midwestern,
friendly to strangers
asking what is good
and where are *you* from
to the cook who sings
"*I want to go home*"
in his nostalgic Country
and Western falsetto.
When a guy in a smoky
the bear hat sneaks in
and says over my shoulder,
"Meet me after chow
at the duty hut, Private."

Dinner hour,
wait for the last man
to arrive at the table.
Drill Sergeant commands,
"Ready seat. Bow your head.
Pray. Now get out you're done."
We eat while standing in line
waiting to shove
our dishes in the
dishroom window.

They feed us well
liver and onions,
part raw with fine flour
part burnt, and steak
country fried chicken
mashed potatoes and gravy
peas, carrots, corn, lots
of veggies, cakes, breads
anything to drink
from the soda fountain
and as much as you want.
There are rumors the best
chow hall is in Kaneohe Bay
Hawai'i. On Sundays they
will charbroil you a steak
outdoors, cooked to order.

Always something new
on the Marine Corps menus,
but regular chow too
pizza and spaghetti
with angel hair pasta
a Wednesday special.

Old Corps Tales

Staff Sgt. Butler's Tale

The mean, green eyed DI said he was fighting in the Tet
and a Chinese officer pulled out his saber waving it high in
the air and led the charge against the hill Sgt. Butler
was defending. That officer was bigger than a Chicago
Bears linebacker, and he was all coked up, thousands of
screaming soldiers ran behind. When Sgt. Butler fired
he hit him in the leg, but the guy was full of cocaine so
he was unphased continued to run closer. Butler shot him
blowing away part of his arm. He kept running, and Sgt.
Butler did not believe his eyes. How could he still be
coming? When the Chinese officer reached a few yards off
Sgt. Butler pulled an illegal weapon made in the USA a
12 gauge shotgun and blew him in half.

The Recruiter's Tale

Devil Dogs, Leathernecks, Jarheads, a few names you will be
called if *you* join. The recruiter rocks back in his chair, takes
a Camel nonfilter, lights it, and inhales. Yeah, I enlisted,
and went to basic. It was tough. This was the *Old Corps*. During
rifle inspection the inspecting officer found a tiny grain of
sand, a speck, in the barrel of a rifle, and that poor devil
had his thumb shoved into the bore and the officer slammed the
M-14 bolt home, and crushed his thumb. Another Jarhead failed
rifle inspection, had to sleep with his rifle a whole week.
The way I toss the truth around, who would believe me? Most
recruits think I am using reverse psychology making up these
stories to try and discourage them from signing up. Being a
Marine is a 24 hour a day job. This is hard, when you sign up
nobody knows what will happen, Vietnam is hell. You might not
make it. Oh, you want to join. Sign right here. Three years
and now I want to send you to St. Louis for a test battery,
and your physical. If you pass we'll write to you, then 1
October report here, Springfield. You recruits will bus to
Saint Louis, fly to San Diego Marine Corps Recruit Depot, MCRD.
After your basic training is complete you'll be one of the proud,
the few, a Marine.

The Sergeant Major's Tale

A Lance Corporal was sent over to my office from the Chaplain
who had asked me to cut orders for the young Marine, and I have
over a hundred clerks working for me here at Camp Pendleton.
My office, the largest on base, my desk all the way to the rear,
we work in one large room. On the white board up in back in
alphabetical order, the list of every Marine Base in the world.
So the Lance Corporal comes in, stands in front of me, I ask
him to look at the board and tell me where he would like me
to send him. Well, he looks at the board, his eyes as big as
a parachute opening, and he says he is a Ground Radio Repairman
and he wants to work in an Electronics Shop. Since there is
one just two blocks away he wants me to cut his orders for there.
Why, he could get his things out of his locker and carry them
to his new job. So that is where I cut his orders. They put
him in charge of their Radio Battery Shop, then six months later,
I cut orders for him to the Marine Airbase Kaneohe Bay Hawai'i.

Junk on the Bunk

Inspection
all of your
possessions
on your bed.
exactly regimented
boots spit shined
brass polished, rifle
clean not a grain of
sand a loose thread
or a wrinkle.
All in order
by the book
you stand at
attention while
an officer looks
down the bore
of your weapon.
Breathe a sigh as he
and the DI walk away.
Happy to have passed,
but one recruit
the highest score
in all events
will win honors
get a promotion
a free set of dress blues,
and on Graduation Day
he will lead the platoon
carrying the guidon.

The Gates of Heaven are Guarded by United States Marines

—Marine Hymn

In training we are
being taught to
have clear vision
as the eagle, to have
sensitive hearing as
the deer, to detect
a scent as the bear.
Jet planes fly overhead
and land every 15 minutes
at San Diego airport.
It is quiet.
I rest on my back,
listen for the chime
of hourly mission bells
to ring their nightly beauty.
Across the bay, in the distance
lights shine on the coast.
Moving toward shore
pacific waves curl surf
uncurl and wash foam
along the beach.
The foam recedes leaving
clumps of rubbery seaweed.

Wild horses in the
saltwater spray.
A fragrance of
eucalyptus boughs.

Duty Hut

Knock three times
and the DI begins to bark,
"100 bend and thrusts."

In this exercise you
bend over touching
your hands, thrust
your legs into a push up
position, bring
your legs back and stand.

This is my discipline
for talking in chow line.

After 100,
"Sir, the Private is done Sir."
DI said
"You are a liar.
You could not have done 100
in that amount of time."

He wants to know my service
number, wants me to
do 2630426
bend and thrusts.

Covered with sweat
and sand
I am doing bend and thrusts.

DI sits with his
feet up on the desk
sips a Pepsi
barks out, "You can go."

Calling Home

An old salt
Staff Sgt. Baker
was calling cadence
marching the platoon
across the drill field,
that same field,
made famous by
Gomer Pyle.

In perfect step
a precision machine
75 men settled down
marching from the waist
making every turn
every heel strike
then Sgt. Baker
called, "halt stand at ease.

Platoon attention.
Any man that wants to
call home, fall out."
He marched them
a few yards away.
He told them it was a
reward for their excellent
drill. Sgt. Baker said,
"because you are from
the St. Louis area
face east, call as loudly
as you can, HOME HOME HOME."

We heard them shouting
"HOME HOME HOME."
We heard Sgt. Baker who said,
"No answer, I guess nobody
is home. Now get back
in rank. Platoon FORWARD MARCH."
Some of us had a good chuckle.

Watering the Grass

Sand sand everywhere
and not a blade of grass,

carrying water by moonlight
splashing we all go.

We go with our bucket
to the head,

as it is our habit
before bed.

Every square inch around
our quonset hut we water

watering the grass, the grass,
this imaginary grass.

Reveille

Usually came before sunrise
dress go to the bathroom
brush your teeth fall in
for roll call, and march
to morning chow,
afterwards every day
we went back to our
barracks to rake the grass.

Sand, sand everywhere
and not a blade of grass.
Furrowed rows of wet sand
raked to imitate cultivated
midwestern cornfields,
as seen from a jumbo jet.

Every square inch around
our quonset huts we raked,
raking the grass, the grass,
this imaginary grass.

Never was any damn grass there,
but every night we water
and every morning we rake.
A part of their mind game,
and we laugh at this foolishness
and try to keep hope alive
because the grass died long ago.

Orders

Staff Sgt. Baker
everybody respected
his integrity.

He played the role
of the loving father.
With his heart

like gold, tried by fire.
In the eighth week
practicing rifle drill

after supper, after dusk,
Sgt. Baker halted us
gave the order, "at ease."

Told those of us that had
cigarettes, and wanted to
could light them up.

He began to shoot the
bull with us privates,
then he paused, and with

a tear in his eye, said
he had orders for Nam.
This was his last day

I have not heard of
or seen Sgt. Baker
after that evening.

Gaslamp

The smoking lamp is lit.
Form two lines facing in,
if you do not smoke
you are the designated ash tray
and must carry your bucket
up and down the rows
until the smoking lamp goes out.

The smoking lamp is lit,
always made me think
of the 1800's gaslamp street lights.
At night somebody had to light them;
come morning somebody put them out.
If you've got them light them up.
The smoking lamp is lit,
always made me think
of Jerome Rothenburg's
"All I want's a good five cent cigar."

The smoking lamp is lit.
The smoking lamp is lit.
The smoking lamp is lit.

Note, each year there are 425,000
smoking related deaths in the USA.
If we lost those Americans in battle
we'd decide to win, or withdraw.

The Wreck of the Hesperus

Are you the wreck
of the Hesperus,
or what? Have you
ever fired a weapon?

I have fired
a Winchester 12 gauge
hunting with friends
on Illinois fields.

I doubted if Marine green eyed
Butler the DI
had read Longfellow
as he took me by surprise

with his direct question
right after I had
come out of sickbay
with five immunizations.

Earlier we marched
in white tee shirts
past fragrant rows of
eucalyptus trees without

being told where we were going.
Marines do not have Medics.
Naval officers and Sailors
staff our sickbay.

Sailors hate Marine recruits and
they were not gentle
at immunization time.
The biggest guys all fainted.

Five shots at once
is a shock. We carried
the big guys out,
then Sergeant Butler

called me over to him
and asked if I was
"The Wreck of the Hesperus,"
had I fired a weapon?

He sent me to the back of the line
to take those five shots again.
A Marine went in, we marched
one step closer to the door.

Some Marines are carried out
with their arms streaming blood.
I do not think I can stand
five more shots, but I stay in line.

It is the game they play
with your mind, to find out
if they can break you,
or at what point you will not

follow an order. As the last man
in front of me went through the door
Sgt. Butler told me to, "get in formation."
In formation, I am the morning star.

The Marine Corps Band

Grandfathers and grandmothers
mothers and fathers and children
are in the grandstand watching
the United States Marine Corps Band.
Perhaps my wife, mother and daughter . . .
their lionhearted faces solemnly
looking over the long drill field.
Unfolding the flag at morning colors,
the sharp creases of red, white and blue
uniforms as if the flag had come to life.
The flag is the length and width of the band.
Rippling in the wind. Raised up the flagstaff.
As the band begins to play and march,
precision marching, rows turn inside
reversing while playing bright anthems
marching in opposite directions.
Soft resonance of our National Anthem
sharp drumbeat of Marine Corps hymn
moving quick step pace across the field,
brilliant military music grows softer
in the distance as they march away
and the visitor crowd disperses.

Drill Sergeant and Recruit Chorus

DRILL SERGEANT

Sound off.

RECRUITS

Sound off.

DRILL SERGEANT

One, two, three-four.

RECRUITS

One, two, three-four.

DRILL SERGEANT

I don't know, but I've been told.

RECRUITS

I don't know, but I've been told.

DRILL SERGEANT

The streets of heaven are lined with gold.

RECRUITS

The streets of heaven are lined with gold.

Running

75 recruits ran
along the beach
in San Diego a slow
group moving in step
their DI jogging backwards.
Some recruit named
Gene Autry sang cadence.
"Amen" was his best.
Six, seven, eight miles,
sand sun sweat pacific,
I always kept pace,
clapped and sang along,
"Everywhere we go
people want to know
who we are
so we tell them
we are the Marine Corps
mighty mighty Marine Corps."

Steve Lowe

We were in Boy Scouts,
and High School.
He was a fun person
he drove God's own blue Chevy;
at the drive-in-burger joint
we talked through our car windows.
He was drafted. I enlisted.
When we got back
we would get together there
and talk about our experiences.
I was out raking the grass,
the third week of training,
I saw him march by in a platoon.
I ran to the end of the barracks
right beside him and
called out his name.
I saw him for the last time.
He was a casualty.
His name, Steve Lowe, forever
on that black stone wall—
the memorial in Washington.

Next to of Course
God, Country, Corps

Why me? Why the Corps?
I had something to prove
raised by my mother
a couple of fading ridged
images of dad in my memory.
I felt I needed discipline,
and I needed the Marine Corps.

Here was the whole spectrum of men.
There were fat boys and skinny boys;
there was the guy who swallowed a needle
trying to get out; there was the guy
who would shit in his bucket every night
who did get out. At the other end
of the spectrum, a couple of guys were
perfect at everything, and handsome too.
I fell somewhere in-between and when
Drill Sergeant yelled "Fall In"
I had my place, my own point of view,
I was a color in the rainbow.

In Scouts our Scoutmaster
Jerry Lowe, Steve Lowe's uncle
was a Marine Sergeant. At night
clouds floated past the moon
on a camping trip. I saw him
press his trousers under the
mattress on his cot over night,
then when he woke up
he had sharp creases.
He was my role model.

There were a lot of good
people who became Marines.
I did learn self-discipline,
and I found that real virtue
came from inside of you.

Fat Boys and Skinny Boys

At chow 300 pound boys
were paired up with
boys that were under 150.
The smaller always got
all of the fat boys'
potatoes, bread and cake.

I was always paired
with a heavy body and
mostly they were jolly
good natured guys,
the kind you would
want to have beside you
in battle.

One recruit was mean as hell
always mad at the skinny
boy that got to eat his
potatoes, bread and cake.
He growled and grumbled
was never really able to
do anything about his loss.

By the end most fat boys
had lost 30 to 40 pounds.
The angry guy lost 60
and got down to 240
so that all the Marines
that were happy graduates
from basic training
weighed 140 to 250.
A lean mean fighting machine.

Absolute Nothing

Sergeant Major, three stripes up
four rockers down with a star.

Master Sergeant, three stripes up
three rockers down with a bursting bomb.

Gunnery Sergeant, three stripes up
two rockers down with crossed rifles.

Staff Sergeant, three stripes up
one rocker down with crossed rifles.

Sergeant, three stripes up
with crossed rifles.

Corporal, two stripes up
with crossed rifles.

Lance Corporal, one stripe up
and crossed rifles.

Private First Class,
one stripe up.

Private,
absolute nothing.

These are the enlisted ranks
of the United States Marine Corps.

Each hash mark on the forearm
right sleeve is four years of service.

Gentlemen, we do not
salute these fighting men,

you salute
officers.

Mail Call

The only contact
you have with a
world outside of
Marine Corps Recruit
Depot San Diego,
you sit on the deck
around Gunnery Sergeant
Sentinella our
platoon commander,
he rocks back
on his chair calling
out the names of those
fortunate few who will
receive mail from home.
Pity the recruit that
receives a stick of gum,
he gets to chew wrapper
and all. If it is a pack,
Gunnery Sergeant Sentinella
makes him distribute it
to his friends, and they
also get to chew wrapper
and all. He was always
laughing, enjoying our
misery and the power he held.
Heaven forbid your sweetheart,
or wife, sends a letter with
sweet smelling perfume
because he rocks back
and rubs the letter in
his crotch, then calls
your name. He always sniffs

each letter until he finds
one that smells good and
smiles, and calls the Corps
the crotch says we are all
in the crotch.

A Marine is a Rifleman First

Marines at weapons training
have to learn how to assemble
and lock and load every weapon.
There are more than a thousand
sorry faced recruits gathered
from the third battalion. All
their lips have been sunburnt,
turned down at the corners
into a typical recruit frown.
On stage our instructor barks
out nomenclature, the military
names of weapon parts.
First he scares hell out of you
making you imagine an enemy wave
in black pajamas at midnight
running when your weapon jams
in the attack. Chaos. The lights go.
You have 45 seconds. Tear it down,
clear out the jam, and reassemble.
Total darkness in the lecture hall.
Now you know you will get
hammered when a weapon jams
in the field. In a fire fight
this rifle is your life.

I Fear No Evil

Helmet, bayonet, flak jacket,
camouflage jungle utilities,
the reality of what you get
twentyfive miles of force
marching, camping, eating cold
C rations out of the can,
crawling under barbed wire
fifty caliber water cooled
machine guns firing over
your head, so if you sit up
you get cut in half and you
crawl in the dirt on your back.
Or sick as a dog you wish you
would die after three days at
sea, rocking side to side, up
and down, rocking and rolling.
Or practicing a beach assault
six thousand Marines landing,
never so happy to set foot
on land, loving that good earth.
And resting during smoking lamp.
Most of these guys write graffiti
on helmets used for their pillow,
"even though I walk through the valley
of the shadow of death, I fear no evil,"
that's what's written there—
like a prayer for courage—
where they rest their heads
and snooze.

At The Head

With green socks
tied around my knees,
a towel, a shaving kit
in my hand, flip-flop
shower shoes, gray P.E. shorts
I am marching in my platoon
as we go to the head to
shit, shower and shave.
Each night the DI on duty
gives us ten minutes
for these three tasks.
While we shower we wash our socks.

Here are four urinals,
two rows of sinks
with mirrors,
two rows of toilets
an open shower room,
plenty of hot water.
This is our most important
competition because
if we have to go again
we must wait for an hour
after taps and miss sleep.
If we miss places when we shave
the DI will dry shave our face,
as we leave the head
with our clean wet socks
tied around our knees.

Corps Sculpting

Thoughts splinter
genesis is a woman
somehow planets were created
sunlight reflecting off them
a steady glow at night
at home some young teen-ager
is pregnant waiting for her good man
to come back from basic
and marry her in his uniform.

Red yellow blue
circle square circle
shapes and found objects
gathered under the western sky
velociraptor and giant insects
a centenarian land turtle
a sea turtle flying through space
the lone star of the Brigadier General
who is a fighter pilot
this corps sculpting
shines in the sunlight.

Hollywood Nightmare

A bad dream comes back
like a comet this nightmare
with a broad tail swooshing
across the stars bits of ice
streaming fire and the dream
rips through your brain like that
until you wake in a cold sweat.
What was the dream about you might ask,
well imagine you are a Marine recruit
at San Diego Marine Corps Recruit Depot MCRD.
You are standing in line at receiving
where people are screaming for clothing
sizes, and all types of clothing are
flying in the air at you, but you are
a Corporal discharged at San Francisco,
honorably, with a good conduct medal.
When in the nightmare you realize
you are back at the starting point
receiving a clothing issue, and going
through basic over, and over again.
And because your training takes place
in Southern Cal., all other Marines
refer to you as a Hollywood Marine,
and this is a Hollywood nightmare.
Comet with a broad tail swooshing,
what is your waist size you puke?

Peace

Marines all go to church
on Sunday there are services
papers signed at enlistment
determined the service and faith
of each recruit. If you were Jewish,
Catholic, Christian, nondenominational,
all have their own meeting time.
Those going to my service
march with me to the auditorium.
For one whole hour each week
the DI cannot yell anything at you.
Most recruits are falling asleep.
Some are snoring, it is hard not to.
Vigorous activities, you are pushed through
in one hour regimented blocks daily,
until you sit in the plush red chair
and listen to the monotone minister
whose words lull you to drowsiness,
and the chair swallows your consciousness.
If you manage to stay awake the irony
of the message is from Romans 14:19
"let us then pursue what makes for peace
and for mutual upbuilding." Marines are
all for that, then at Sunday dinner bell
some of those more devout Devil Dogs
growl, "pass the fucking pepper."

Rifle Salute

Another high school buddy
fell in love and married.
His young wife became pregnant.
He was such a cautious driver
when she was in the car 45 mph
was as fast as he would go.
One day he was rolling along
at 45 mph when his car
blew a tire, the door opened,
his bride was thrown out
a wheel pinned her stomach.
She died in his arms.
He joined the Marines.
He volunteered for
three back to back
duty tours in Nam.
Now a rifle salute
seven Marines, three volleys
will honor his burial.

He Was a Car Thief

He was good. He could steal a car in less than a minute.
He'd taken 15 cars when he got caught: the Judge told him
he could go to prison, or join the Marine Corps for six
years. He was the happiest Marine. He wore his uniform with
pride. The Corps straightened out his life, and he was
happily married. A tall blond man with blue eyes, a new
life and many new friends. Everybody was amazed to hear
his story.

So You Want Out

If you wanted
out of basic
training, out
of the Marines,
the DI told us
to get off base
wait until after
midnight, take a
blanket, when the
firewatch was at
the far end of camp
make a run for it.
Throw the blanket
over the barbedwire,
hop over, and you
are in downtown
San Diego, simple.

If the Shore Patrol
catch you they throw
you in the brig.

If you wanted
out of life,
out of this world
altogether, then
cut your wrists
up and down the
arteries and veins,
do it in the shower.

If the suicide attempt
does not work you
are going to sickbay
until you are well,
then back on the
yellow footprints
for training at
square one again.

Trying to Get Out

A Private
swallowed
a needle.

He thought
he could get out.

Thought the Corps
would let him go.

Our DI let him
lay in his bed
three days,

then sent him
back to duty.

Another Private

He used the
blanket method.

We never saw him,
nor heard of him.

He went
AWOL.

Relieving Himself

Late at night
he would
shit in his
bucket.

Recruits
in his hut
complained.

For a week
he shit in
his bucket.

The Corps
let him out.

Killing in 8 Seconds

In hand to hand combat
we are taught to kill.
Not only to kill, but
to demoralize the enemies'
will to fight. Instead of
taking a prisoner, pull
out their eyes and crush
them on their chest,
send them back to their
friends to show what happens
if they get caught.
Or to kill somebody
in eight seconds, grab
the enemies throat
snap their larynx.
With that pulled out
you cannot breathe
and you suffocate.

The Firewatch Ribbon

That first night we were told not to go outside because
there were armed guards. They turned out to be recruits
wearing orange vests, carrying flashlights on firewatch
duty. They wake you at midnight and send you out to a post
to walk the beat a couple of hours, and they tell you to
say, "halt who goes there," to anybody that comes along.
The hard part is staying awake. Everybody in the Marines
during the Viet Nam era was awarded the National Defense
ribbon. It was the big joke that was called the firewatch
ribbon, earned by walking firewatch. In the Marines two
things were certain: you'll walk firewatch, and you'll
have a National Defense ribbon. Actually it was pretty
red and yellow, white and blue, worn above the rifle medal.
All other medals, Purple Hearts, Bronze and Silver Stars,
were combat earned. An unusual moment in time, firewatch.

Famous Marines

Walt Disney proudly
displayed his Dishonorable
Discharge on the wall
of his office behind him
when he talked on his show.

Steve McQueen stole a tank
painted it pink and drove
down the main street in Oceanside
and they gave him a Dishonorable.

John Wayne played the role
of jarhead in the movies
a real Hollywood marine
he was so well loved
real marines idolized him.

Rumors

We were sitting around
on our footlockers
spit polishing our boots
cleaning our rifles
and writing letters home
when Staff Sgt. Butler
came in and said that
Paul McCartney of the
Beatles was dead,
sending shock waves
of depression through
us all. First John Kennedy,
Bobby, Dr. King and now Paul.
When would it ever stop?
Sgt. Butler said the papers
only had rumors. He was
barefoot on the album jacket
while the other lads wore shoes,
a symbol of his death, and nobody
knew exactly where he was.
Newspapers, magazines and TV
stations had the same rumors.
Paul McCartney of the Beatles
rock and roll band was dead.
That night we were all sad
when the lights went out;
our hearts were listening
when the bugle sounded taps.

Private in Another Platoon

Never bothered him
when the DI would call
him names, yell in his face,
or say that he was the worst
recruit they had ever seen
or heard tell of, he never
showed them any fear at all.
They pulled him aside and took
him out behind the duty hut
and asked him why he never showed
any fear when they started in
screaming and threatening him.
He said, "it was just like
being at home, Sir. Just like
the Private's home life."

The DI asked him to pretend
he was afraid and to play
the game because he was bringing
down the whole system. Couldn't he
just fake it a little? And then,
they sent him back and left him
alone after that, except when
they caught him talking to another
recruit when he should have been
cleaning his rifle. They beat him up
and he promised to return the beating
if he ever saw them again after basic.
You have to keep your rifle clean
in order to hit the target at the range.
It is important to qualify as Marksman,
Sharpshooter, or Expert.

Lewis B. Puller, Lt. General

Jupiter has four moons
discovered by Galileo.
Chesty Puller has five
Navy Crosses, the second
highest medal awarded
to a Marine.

Chesty fought four wars
and other battles
where U.S. Marines landed.

Once when surrounded
by an enemy he told his men,
"those poor bastards, they've got
us right where we want them."

An Army battalion
lost half their men
fighting through to them.
When he showed their officer
the line on the perimeter
to attack

their officer asked
where the troops
could fall back
if they were overrun.
Chesty got on the radio
to his artilleryman,
"if they move back a foot
shoot them."

Dog-eared

There was something
romantic about the Marines.
A book I'd read about leathernecks
at the battle of Peleliu
I found captivating.
Chesty Puller was C.O.
in one of the bloodiest
battles on a little island
in World War Two, then Captain
John N. McLaughlin was awarded
the Silver Star for gallantry
there. He later became Major General,
our Commanding General, at Marine Corps
Recruit Depot, where we were trained.
Robert Leckie wrote his book
from his personal experience
the book was titled *A Helmet
for my Pillow*; my friends
read, passed around and around,
until that book was dog-eared.
And I read the book last
I know this because I kept it.
I treasured that paperback.
There were wounds, pain and malaria,
we read the book at MacMurray
College's student union. Our
local high school hangout.
The Esprit de Corps first
touched me in that place.

John N. McLaughlin, Major General

The Commanding General. Once in a while we would see
his car go by from the drill field. We knew it was the
Commanding General by those red flags with two gold stars
riffling on the wind as he whooshed by; it was not until
later we would find out that he fought gallantly at Peleliu,
and that in the Korean war he was held captive three years
by the Chinese. When finally released he was awarded the
legion of merit given for exceptionally meritorious conduct.
During peace time he excelled in several positions state-
side, and he earned a Master's Degree in International
Affairs at George Washington University. By 1967 he was
C.O. of the 6th Marines, 2nd Marine Division and was pro-
moted from Colonel to Brigadier General earning a Gold Star
in lieu of his second legion of Merit—while in Viet Nam—
he became the Assistant Division Commander of the 1st Marine
Division; he was promoted to Major General September 1969
and assigned to MCRD San Diego as Commanding General. I
arrived there a raw recruit standing on the yellow footprints
October 1, 1969.

Phase Two

Edson Rifle Range at Camp Pendleton

Up until now we carried our rifles on the drill field.
We learned how to do left shoulder and right shoulder
arms, parade rest, salute, and in general how to tear
down, clean vigorously, and reassemble our rifles. When
we got to Edson we had classes on how to hold, sight
and fire the M-14 weapon. This was the most important
part of training. In battle that weapon would keep you
alive. You needed to know how to fire and there are three
medals for recruits who qualify at the range. This two
week training period divided men, who would be Marines,
from boys. Your first medal: Marksman, Sharpshooter, or
Expert awarded. In two short weeks *you* would be tested;
you would fire your weapon at the range. The totals,
hits and bullseyes on the target would determine if you
qualified. "If you do not qualify—you had better give
your soul to God, because your ASS belongs to me," our
Drill Instructor threatened, and he was serious this time.
The third phase of Marine Basic is hell for recruits who
do not qualify. Remember, a Marine is a rifleman first.

Intimate Dust

Fresh born like ducklings
eleven following their mother-hen,
we hike a dirt trail
following our Drill Instructor
in two columns with M-14 rifles
slung over our shoulders.
At the range we form a giant circle
for snapping in, or getting into shape
for shooting. We stretch
and take different positions
hours and hours we practice
prone and sitting, in the dirt,
intimately holding our weapons
with the straps around our hands, the
riflebutts tight against our shoulders
looking down the cold barrels
at the sights, and at the
imaginary targets, that poor slob,
the recruit opposite us in the circle.
This is the wild wild west.
The Pacific coast in the background
buzzards with their six foot wing span
circling overhead, rising in the heat.
By 21:30 I'm in the lower bunk
because at the range our day begins
at 03:30. Every muscle and
tendon ached as taps played.
DI turns off the lights, the sky
twilight, an arrival of stars
as we sing deeply the Marine Hymn,
and say our prayers, and go to
sleep. Our whole platoon in one room

with row after row of bunkbeds
in the new barracks. Our DI, spitpolished,
in his best dress uniform, rifle medal,
ribbons, recon wings, a killer smile,
going out for his night of liberty.

Snapping In

Pain is good
no pain, no gain
pain is impurities
leaving the body.
Circles of circles
get up at three-thirty
eat morning chow
hike to class
at Edson Range.
Most Marines in
the Japanese theater
during WWII had this
same training course.
We have our friend the M-14.
We have our shooting jackets.
Seated at the outdoor bleachers,
we are listening to instruction.
For a whole week
there are circles,
lying, sitting, standing,
stretching muscles
we did not know we had,
before stretching.
Hour after hour
seven days of snapping in.
Try to enjoy the silence
because next week
we'll have live ammo.
We'll shoot at circles
on targets 500 yards away,
then we'll shoot
to qualify for a medal.

Right now, impurities
are leaving the body
no pain, no gain
pain is good.

We Are Elements of Stars

Those stories you have heard
about Marines cleaning bathrooms
with toothbrushes, and the commander
checking places for dust
wearing a white glove, checking
ledges above doors, and pipes
and air vents, or a DI bouncing
quarters off bunkbeds to see if
they were made with military folds,
all of it is true. They made us
get up by 3:30 a.m.
to clean the head until it sparkled
to clean the floors to make our beds,
and then go to morning chow,
then hike to snapping in class.
We marched to chow in pitch dark.
The great thing was we could
see the stars at four a.m.
I could see the Milky Way
galaxy with thousands of stars.
A cloud of stars perfectly clear;
we are made of the same elements.

Outstanding

Liver and onions
are what we had to eat
for dinner.
The pressures here
were more relaxed.
The emphasis was on
learning to shoot accurately,
running and meticulous
cleaning of the floors and heads.
During our free time
in the evening we could
write letters home,
or shower and shave. I was
leaving the shower last
holding my shaving kit
in one hand, holding
a towel around my waist
with the other
standing there in my flip-flops
when the bantamweight DI and
my DI Sgt. Butler came in
and halted me
to play a little game
punching me
to see who could knock me back
further. I braced when they punched;
they both hit me three times.
Neither was able to knock me back a step.
They said I was outstanding.
Our showers were on the same
floor as their office,
and a glass wall divided

them from our living quarters.
Was I fortunate
to keep my liver and onions down?
The center of my chest turned scarlet.

Marksman

Would there be hell to pay
if you did not qualify
at Edson Rifle Range?
Not really. There were
over twenty recruits
in my platoon who failed
to qualify with the M-14,
the weapon of WWII. We had to
learn that weapon first, although
what we would use in Viet Nam
was the M-16 affectionately known
as the matty-mattel a plastic stock.
Recruits who failed in Marine Basic
they were yelled at a little more,
given work detail a little more,
expected to do better
in every Marine area
a little more, while
those of us who did qualify
could relax and celebrate because
we had earned our first medal,
and were we cool, or what?
A few had earned Marksman.
That medal was affectionately
known as the toilet seat.
Then there was Sharpshooter
a medal that was a Silver Cross.
The best was Expert rifleman
represented by crossed rifles.
These medals were worn
only on the dress uniform
directly below the National

Defense ribbon. You might be curious
as to which medal I received,
mine was the toilet seat.

Running Test

There are gentle rolling
foothills in California
wide spaces open for runs,
and our platoon goes out
for long slow group running.
Private Kennedy carried
our crimson pennant 3183
with a white flag below
with a black panther leaping
and these words, "Sent From Hell."
We go on runs of seven,
eight, or nine miles.
These runs most everybody
looks forward to for exercise,
and we go for morning,
afternoon and evening runs.
In step running side by side,
singing, chanting, clapping,
the DI running backwards
watching us go forward.
In boots, long pants, and
white tee shirts, through
the dust, and the sand.
Down through history
and time disjointed, what
position, like so many before,
and those to come afterwards
to the running test alone.
Running from one post to
the other, two hundred yards
away and back, timed for three
miles through dust, and dehydration.

No quitting, no stops, no resting,
no water for my parched throat,
just running. And mentally to
get through it, the whole way
I sang "Hey Jude" because
back at home the girlfriend
who waited for me was Judy.

Qualification Day

I am a small fighter.
There is a big evil
out there. How can we
stop the evil of our
time with bullets?
Our DI said if anybody
was nervous about firing
at the range he had
some tranquilizers,
gave out two per shooter.
They were gray pills
I popped them into
my mouth and chewed.
They were charcoal
placebo, placebo.
They stuck in the throat.
When it was my turn to shoot
I sighted the bullseye
and began squeezing
the trigger, and no matter
how tight I held the weapon
it pushed my shoulder back.
I squeezed. It pushed.
I knew the kick of firing
from hunting in the Illinois
winter fields with friends.
I had a 12 gauge Winchester
pump action shotgun that
fired three rounds before
reloading. I'd learned
how to hold a rifle against
my shoulder, how to hit

swiftly moving wild game.
These were stationary targets.
I could take my time,
sight and squeeze the trigger.

Saltpeter

Three days nobody in my platoon would eat butter. The rumor
going around was they put saltpeter in butter. Why did they
put saltpeter in our butter? Well, it would prevent us from
getting an erection. We would not want 75 horny 19 year olds
running around. After three days we ate butter. We did not
have radio, TV, VCR, no girls, except in our dreams, eating
was the pleasure they couldn't take away. Our rifle Instruc-
tor told us this rhyme while holding a rifle and his crotch,
"This is my rifle, this is my gun, this is for pleasure, and
this is for fun."

At Midnight

Rainfall is rare
in southern California.
Eight feet high fog
comes in from the Pacific
ocean, crosses the drill field,
then lifts into clouds.
Over my Marine raincoat
I have my orange vest on
because this is my night
for firewatch duty, and
I have a flashlight. I am
walking at midnight.
Streets, rooftops, palm trees,
eucalyptus trees, are wet.
Everything is wet or damp
from a fine mist in the air.
I am comfortable, dry and warm.
I can see the San Diego lights,
the bridge over the bay.
The muse is here with me.
We share this solitude,
and the fresh eucalyptus
on the sweet rain.

The Top Ten Things
Marines Love and Hate

#10
Marines love being
in a large group of men,
they hate not being able
to see any beautiful women.

#9
Marines love being
immersed in their work,
they hate not being able
to go fishing, or watch sports.

#8
Marines love laughing along
with humorous mind games,
they hate being
the butt of the joke.

#7
Marines love wearing
their uniforms with pride,
they hate final inspection day.

#6
Marines love receiving
mail from loved ones,
they hate getting cookies, cupcakes,
and gum, and having to eat them
wrapper and all.

#5
Marines love being alive,
they hate dying in battle.

#4
Marines love being healthy
not getting the flu, or malaria,
they hate getting five
shots at a time from Navy Medics.
Shots make them faint.

#3
Marines love listening
to their Drill Instructor's voice
singing cadence at close order drill,
or telling salty combat stories,
they hate when the DI screams
commands at them barking like a dog.

#2
Marines love to eat mashed
potatoes and gravy, corn-on-the-cob,
peas and carrots, fried chicken, pork chops
and steak, cookies, cake and bread,
they hate when somebody skinny
is permitted to sit beside them
and eat their food.

#1
Marines love graduating from
Basic Training, and they hate that training
has ended that they will not see their
DI in his smoky the
bear hat anymore and wish they
could do it all over, "Go back and
DO IT OVER."

Sunflower and Moonbeam

Twelve weeks seem an eternity
when you are nineteen in Basic
if your girlfriend at home
is pregnant waiting for you,
misery is spending twelve
lonely weeks for the first time
being away from Judy miles apart
and recalling how cute she is
and the sound of her voice when
she would offer, "don't get mad,
get glad," from a pop TV commercial,
and time carries on a frail twig
in an angry river washing downstream.

Knowing not the future
the outcome of that moonbeam love
the sunflower of all the wonderful
days to come full of joy,
knowing not that at forty-six
love might have been something
you did not know you had and
twelve weeks seem a blink
of the eyelash, a wisp of fog.

Light raindrops on a windshield
diamond quality of light
passing through those raindrops
and the gentle sound of soft rain
when were together in the car
in front of Judy's home and we
had to say good-by not wanting
to be separated, that precious moment

etched permanently on my heart,
our daughter Crystal growing strong
and beautiful inside her mother.

Purple Hearts

After you are wounded in action
you are awarded the Purple Heart.

George Washington
his image is on the medal
in the heart shape,
the ribbon is purple.

Some I have known
received the medal and
will not speak of it.

Carefully if you listen
you may hear,

"a scar on the leg, shrapnel."

In Marine Basic Purple
Hearts are not awarded.

Anybody who went to Viet Nam,
their life was changed forever.
Friends who were casualties
they were awarded Purple Hearts.

Avoiding conflict,
how many went to Canada?

Sharpshooter Kisses

I am proud to wear
the Silver Cross on my chest,
the sharpshooter medal.
I am that Marine wearing it
on graduation day.
You know me.
I have seen the eagle fly
in the clearing
along an august marshmallow cloud
gliding the thunderstorm's edge
curve on the wind
then circle back.
In high country
along a fresh ice-melt river
I have stalked a moose
and seen buffalo.
When I fire my weapon
at the rifle range
qualifying day
I adjust for wind,
the minute inaccuracy
in the sight.
When I squeeze the trigger
lead flies like an
eagle in the clearing.

Expert Marksmanship

He is the best
at the range.
He hit center
never far from center
with each shot.
He will be the Marine
you want on your fire team.
He is the guy
you want beside you
in blazing battle.
On his chest
tiny silver crossed rifles
the best shooter.

Perfect sight
and precise
impact on target,
did you ever
wonder with all
those recruits
firing at once—
how do you know
whose bullet
hit which target?
Just a thought.

I requalified,
went from marksman
to expert, although
I didn't feel
any different,

wore those crossed
silver rifles
with pride.

Twilight Hymn

Starlight begins to prick holes in the dark. And night
has its own light in that dusk purple sage. Its the final
skivvies inspection before bed at Edson Range, and all
the nonquals, Marksmen, Sharpshooters, and the Experts
are snug in their racks. Staff Sergeant Butler leads the
cattle lowing caterwauling of the Marine Hymn. The sound
of it is beautiful. Tomorrow, early we'll be on our way
back to MCRD in San Diego. By noon in the blistering sun
we'll march in close order drill across an asphalt surface,
heat falling in light on us like pollen off a sunflower.

Phase Three

Keeping Busy

The Drill Instructors are calling us Marines for the first
time. We are allowed to wear starched and pressed uniforms
with collars unbuttoned at the top, and our trousers bloused
at the top of our boots. We feel and act sharp like Marines
as we go into the final stretch of basic advanced recruit
training. I am glad to have qualified as a marksman at the
range. The DI seems to focus less on those who earned
shooting medals and more on those who did not. These are
the final preparation weeks polishing for graduation.
Every hour in training is planned and structured. With
diligence we work toward graduation day.

What is a Marine?

Marines laugh, cry, sing,
they raise families,
care about humanity
and want everlasting
peace in the world.

A Marine believes in
the United States,
is willing to stand up
and defend the country.

Is it a brotherhood,
a fellowship? Is it
not being willing to
leave anybody behind
in a firefight?

Many have taken up the
title of United States marine
and given their lives
for your freedom.

Men and women too,
that bled bright crimson
if they got wounded.

During a war or
a national emergency
if Marines are not
the first to go
then who is?

They are the President's own
ready for deployment
with 24 hour notice
anywhere on land, on sea,
and in the air

Sand Crabs

Where clouds billow along the beach,
you might observe a sand crab
run sideways into foam,
or hear the gull cry.

"I don't want to see you."
Our Drill Instructor was flustered.
We had all been out of step,
and out of line. That was
the absolute worst we had marched,
in close order drill, since
that first week in boot camp.

So the DI marched us into the sand, sand
consisting of sediment bits
with rough jagged edges,
and shell fragments.
This was a test of our true mettle.
This was humbling.
On our back with our rifle
we had to lay down
and bury ourselves in the sand.

Close Combat

Helmets and pugil sticks
were the great equalizers;
no matter what size you were
nobody could really get hurt.
A pugil stick
was like a giant
cotton swab with
padded gloves
to protect the hands.
We formed a circle in the sand.
The people in the circle
cheered, laughed and
whistled at the mortal combatants.
We had taken our covers off
preparing to put the
white football helmets on.
Here was the shiny skin,
our nearly bald heads.
With a DI on each side
it was kill or be killed.
Everybody had their turn
to attack an opponent.
When my turn came for close combat
I ran forward, screaming
as loud as my lungs would allow,
holding the pugil stick
like a knight's lance.
I caught my opponent
under the chin and
used my legs to thrust
upward as hard as I could.
He was knocked on his butt.

Grunts

Although every Marine
is basically a grunt
that's not what you join for
its what you get.
Drab faded olive green stuff.
Canvas backpack, camouflage
half tent shelter, a belt
with rifle magazine holders,
canteen, bayonet sheath and
bayonet, rifle, and a helmet
also in camouflage, virtually
all you'll need to survive
in the heat of battle and be
a grunt. A member of a team
of guys with mental and moral
qualities dating back to
November 10, 1775. Guys who
are always faithful and use
Semper Fidelis as their motto.
There's a famous monument of
the guys in green, the green
machine, guys raising the
American flag together at
the battle of Iwo Jima.
A grunt has tenacity of attack,
courage and faithfulness.
Some have tattoos of bulldogs.
Grunts are self-sacrificing,
always ready to keep peace.

Final Inspection

Our Gunnery Sergeant Sentinella
is in his full dress uniform
carrying a sword in his right hand
the blade facing forward
the blunt part resting
against his right shoulder
the most stern look
on his face tells us that
this inspection is serious.

Our platoon is aligned
into four squads or lines
in our dress greens
our buckles, shoes and
hat brims polished to
a mirror perfection.
At our right leg our
inspection ready clean
rifle. We stand silent
at attention. Waiting
for a Lieutenant colonel,
a First Lieutenant to
inspect uniform and rifle.

When the Lt. Colonel steps
in front of me, I snap the
rifle up diagonally across
my chest. When he makes a motion
to reach for my weapon I snap
my hands down sharply to my side.
This is the way it is done.
He looks down the barrel

for the slightest speck
of dust or sand, checks
the wooden stock and hands
the weapon back. Now he looks
at my uniform for a loose fit,
thread, or anything out of place.
"Outstanding Marine," he says
turning crisply to the young
man standing next to me.
He grabs his rifle. I breathe
easier. I passed.

Sergeant Neno and the Samoan Sergeant

Sergeant Neno was a popular guy.
He loved the rank of Corporal
because with it came the privilege
of being a noncommissioned officer
without most of the responsibility.
Sergeants had to chat with officers
a lot and pass orders and instructions
along the chain-of-command to the men
of lower ranks below him. Sergeant Neno
did not care for that so every time
he was promoted to Sergeant he would
go to Waikiki beach and vacation there
for a couple of weeks. When he returned
he would be busted to Corporal.

The Samoan Sergeant had snow-white hair.
He had been in the Marine Corps
all of his adult life. He was the
most decorated Marine in WWII, or
so the story was told around base.
He had the Congressional Medal
of Honor and a chest full of ribbons.
He was a Sergeant and an alcoholic.
He was the linen room Sergeant.
A one man job. He took your dirty
sheets, when you brought them,
and gave you two clean sheets.
Every day he drank a six-pack
of Primo for lunch, then on his
way driving home drank another

six-pack of beer, then during
the evening drank two more six-
packs. A case of Primo a day.
He had been busted to Private
several times and would dry out
and work his way back up to Sergeant.
They would never throw him out
because he was a battlefield hero.

Last Hour of Sunlight

At dinner on the last day
of basic I finished early,
went outside the chow hall
to stand, and wait for
the other fellows to finish
eating their dinner.
It was the last hour of
sunlight. The time of day
when sunlight comes at you
from the west, and seems
to wash all around you
leaving a shadow that is
sixty feet going east.
There are three large
chow halls here in a row.
I am alone in the wide open
space. In the cloudless
western sky, a few sea-
gulls hang around for scraps.
This is the first time
I have seen a seagull
up close. The bird
walks right in front
of me, and stops to look
me over. The bird must
think it odd that I am
here all alone, and wonders
if I have any food. When
there is no food the bird
flies to the roof on the
chow hall. Soon a few other
fellows join me standing

in the light. With everybody
here Sgt. Butler calls us
to attention. We turn, "right
face," and begin marching . . .
left foot first, right,
left right, left right, left
right, away from the chow hall.

From the Halls of Montezuma

This is a black and white photograph.
One of the buildings that surround
the drill field. A receiving barracks,
they were all the same with pale yellow
exteriors, and red tile roofs, and halls.
You could walk down the halls like a
porch, and be outside the building, yet
underneath the roof looking ahead.
It was like walking through the halls
of time knowing everybody came into the
Corps and had a similar experience,
a similar feeling. Treasures from home
were lost. Childhoods forever left behind
in material things: baseball card collections,
coin and comicbook collections, bats, gloves,
high school letters, all the mementos
your childhood could gather, including
youthful, smiling friends, were lost.
If you survived, then you would be
a man. There were trees around my homeplace:
an ancient tree-of-heaven, a mature maple,
a gold apple, and a flowering catalpa
that a catbird called home. In the summer
there was a row of peonies and splashes
of colorful tulips in the spring.
And brilliant friends, all had to be left.
You had to look less at the material world
walking down those Marine Corps halls
that black and white photograph,
and ask what was to gain from the loss?
Sometimes a person has a long, long,
amazingly humble walk.

Faces

What do we know
we can take away
from Marine Basic?
Those first two weeks
were orientation.
The DIs tried to scare
us, tear us down, and
put the fear of God
in us, as we became
familiar with the
place and faces.
When it is ended
and we are Marines
working our eight
to five jobs, and
beyond, when we go
back to civilian
life many years
from now, what
will we have
memories of? Faces
with down turned
lips, burnt by
the sun and wind.
Faces that blend
and run together,
a few names
an image here
and there.
The DI
stands alone
adjusts

his cover.
He is waiting
for his next
platoon of faces
to arrive.

Unrest

Inside indoctrination;
outside race riots
and protests anti-war
demonstrations
blood on the gates
citizens beaten by
Chicago police,
the National Guard
shot its own citizens,
students at Kent State.
Outside you have
drugs, alcohol, tobacco.
Inside you have
tobacco; it was killing
us. And we had political
parties spying illegally.
Free love, free sex,
the Beatles were
disillusioned, went up
on a rooftop to make art
by playing their last gig
together, a free concert.
Men walked on the moon.
The flag unfurled,
silk gossamer, waving
in the wind, and the
tides unchanged, went out
and came back in, went
out, and came back in.
And nobody knew what
to do.

Marine Ball

The men wear the same
white hat with a gold
eagle, globe and anchor.
A nehru jacket so deep
navy blue that it looks
black. With gold buttons.
Bright blue trousers with
a wide red stripe
down the outside seam.
Shoes spit polished black
with high gloss.
A stainless steel sword.
The women beautiful
in dinner dresses of
different styles and
elegant colors.
That is what you join for
floating to the music
across the dancefloor
still a contender and
the band plays on every
November 10th, on the
Marine Corps birthday.
Like a harvest moon
floating through clouds,
hung on the ceiling a
ball made of mirrors
spins the light around
and around the floor in
the dark and the music.
A couple goes outside
to sit on the porchswing,

you and your bride-to-be.
A moment they look at
the orange moon, they kiss,
love comes back like love can.

Dreams That Shapeshift

Point blank I knew a Marine Corporal
He went to Electronics School after basic
in San Diego for a whole year.
He thought he wanted to be a
Secret Service Agent, take a
correspondence course in sociology,
the prerequisite for criminology.
He got orders for Hawai'i, tried out
for their fast pitch semipro softball team.
Marine bases had their own teams.
He made the next-to-the-last cut,
began to dream about the big leagues.
It was fun. He was hitting the ball
to the fence and he couldn't believe it.
Also, he was catching balls in center field.
The team was going to keep two players who
would be expected to purchase their own
uniforms. He made the final cut, then
he got sick. He did not buy his uniform,
nor did he play baseball. In the hospital,
they kept him for observations.
After his kidney surgery was successful
he went to work in the Urology Clinic.
I heard he attended Illinois University
majored in anthropology, and writing.

What Were the Three Hardest Things About Marine Basic?

Getting into shape. In the beginning my weight was 115. At the end, after twelve weeks, my weight was 140. Three square meals and regular workouts helped me to gain weight for the first time in my young adult life. If you were an Ohio State college football player, you might be in worse shape after basic because training was not as rigorous as NCAA weight training. The first weeks the USMC tore us down, then they gradually built you back up, but that was never an easy process.

Doing exactly what you were told. Turning left when commanded to and striking your foot down when everybody else did in close order drill with a rifle may look easy, but it is not. Then you were given ten minutes to shit, shower and shave. It became a competition. There were twenty-five toilets, four long urinals, eight shower-heads twenty sinks and you had to learn to go in shifts.

Being away from home. No contact from the world outside, without any comforts of home except for an occasional mail call and reading the Sunday paper was hard. Also, being isolated from family, friends and those you love was hard because in Marine Basic there were no phone calls, no TV, movies, VCR, or girl-friends. And that was the hardest, no girlfriends.

What Were the Three Easiest Things About Marine Basic?

On an overcast day when everything was gray, and cold
I have seen a blazing cross a pink light on the horizon
everything coated with ice. This happened on Thanks-
giving and it made it easy to believe in Jesus.

                              Church
was one of the easiest things in Marine Basic. You sat
in a soft chair in an auditorium listening to a minister's
voice come to put you to sleep, and you would be in a
small town in Illinois on a lazy summer day.

                            Sleeping.
It was absolutely the easiest thing to do. You became so tired
you could sleep standing up, sleep marching. You could sleep
on firewatch duty. When your head hit the pillow in fifteen
minutes you were in dream land dreaming about food.

                              Eating.
Eating Thanksgiving dinner. All that delectable mouthwatering
food. Eating was always easy because I got extra potatoes, bread
and cake. The tables were spread with a Thanksgiving day feast
and we thanked Jesus, ate heartily and then rested.

The Fighter Pilot

This fighter jet
curves in space
in front of you
a green camouflage.
Roaring like a lion
soaring through august clouds.
He might be a fighter pilot.
A one star General
waking up in the hospital
bed beside you.
He might laugh
and tell you
he likes to wear his hair short
because it is cool under his helmet,
his white pilot helmet.
The fighter pilot
might be recovering
from kidney surgery
on the same day as you.
This might be real
or it might be a dream.

Two Creeds

Drill Instructor's Creed:
These are my recruits.
I will train them
to the best of my ability.
I will develop them into
smartly disciplined,
physically fit, basically
trained Marines, thoroughly
indoctrinated in love
of God, country and corps.
I will demand of them and
demonstrate by my own example,
the highest standards of
personal conduct, morality
and professional skill.

The Recruit's Creed:
To be a Marine
you have to believe in
yourself, your fellow Marine
your corps, your country, your God,
semper fidelis.

Graduation

In the night sky Cassiopeia, Cygnus, Draco and the Big
Dipper visible. Last night we saw those together; looking
at constellations like connect the dots. Graduation is
the brightest sun shining, gooseflesh jubilant, shouting
for joy day in my life. In the morning we showered, put
on our best dress uniform and prepared to march together
that one last time to our rite of passage ceremony. Our
faces beaming hope, our creases sharp, when Gunnery Ser-
geant Sentinella called, "PLA — TOON 3183, FALL — IN."
Marching at the front of the platoon was Private First
Class Kennedy wearing the Honor Blues, carrying a guidon
with our flag marching beside Gunny Sentinella who carried
his Marine sword. Four platoons were graduating and in
silence we listened for our C.O. at long last to say,
"Congratulations Marines."

We shouted, jumped up and down, and tossed our covers
into the leatherneck, jarhead, devildog, sky. Then, one-
by-one shook hands with our DI whose olive green stripes
were crossing on the field of red.

About the Author

• Born March 1950 in
Jacksonville, Illinois

• Served in the U.S. Marine
Corps 1969–1972

• Received BA from University of Illinois, Springfield

• Earned MA in English
Literature/Creative
Writing at the University
of Colorado in Boulder

• Published *American
Western Song* in 2000

Victor W. Pearn

Photo by Dale Hicks

• Nominated twice for Pulitzer Prize in Poetry

• Father of four daughters and grandfather of three granddaughters

• Has given and continues to provide poetry readings at public libraries,
universities, conferences, etc. Please contact the author for readings and
workshops at happypoet@hotmail.com